Cystic Fibrosis

By Judy Monroe

Consultant:
Marlyn S. Woo, MD
Director, The Cystic Fibrosis Center,
Childrens Hospital Los Angeles
Associate Professor of Pediatrics,
Keck School of Medicine
at University of Southern California

Perspectives on Disease and Illness

LifeMatters
an imprint of Capstone Press
Mankato, Minnesota

LifeMatters books are published by Capstone Press
PO Box 669 • 151 Good Counsel Drive • Mankato, Minnesota 56002
http://www.capstone-press.com

Printed in the United States of America

Library of Congress Cataloging-in-Publication Data
Monroe, Judy.
    Cystic fibrosis / by Judy Monroe.
        p.   cm. — (Perspectives on disease and illness)
    Includes bibliographical references and index.
    ISBN 0-7368-1026-9
    1. Cystic fibrosis—Juvenile literature. [1. Cystic fibrosis.] I. Title. II. Series.
    RC858 .C95 M66 2002
    616.3´7—dc21

00-012612
CIP

    Summary: Discusses what cystic fibrosis is and how it affects the body; also explains how the disease is diagnosed and managed currently and how it may be managed in the future; includes information on finding support and living with the condition.

Staff Credits
Rebecca Aldridge, editor; Adam Lazar, designer and illustrator; Kim Danger, photo researcher
Interior production by Stacey Field

Photo Credits
Cover: ©Artville/Don Carstons, left; RubberBall, middle; ©Digital Vision, right;
The Stock Market/©Howard Sochurek, bottom
©Artville, 41
©Digital Vision, 22, 27
International Stock/©Dusty Willison, 32; ©James Davis, 38; ©Scott Barrow, 47; ©Michael Agliolo, 49
©Marlyn S. Woo, MD, 31
Photo Network/©Fabricius & Taylor, 8; ©Myrleen Ferguson Cate, 43; ©Esbin-Anderson, 48;
©Eric R. Berndt, 52
©Stockbyte, 7
Uniphoto/Pictor/25, ©Larry Merkle, 18; ©Jackson Smith, 34, 59
Visuals Unlimited/©Kim Fennema, 17

A 0 9 8 7 6 5 4 3 2 1

Table of Contents

Chapter Overview

Cystic fibrosis is a serious, chronic, and usually deadly disease. It affects thousands of people worldwide.

Cystic fibrosis is a genetic disease. It is inherited, or passed down through each parent.

Cystic fibrosis can affect people of any race. However, it is more common among Caucasians than any other ethnic group.

The respiratory system is hit the hardest in people with cystic fibrosis. These people often have difficulty breathing and get many lung infections. People with cystic fibrosis usually have problems with their digestive system and sweat glands, too. Cystic fibrosis often affects the reproductive system of males who have the disease.

Cystic fibrosis was first recognized as a disease in the United States in 1938. For many years, doctors did not understand that cystic fibrosis affected many body systems.

Chapter 1

What Is Cystic Fibrosis?

"You have cystic fibrosis, Glenn."
Dr. Martin's words echoed through
Glenn's head. Glenn looked at her mother.

Glenn, Age 14

"That's impossible," said her mother. "Our first doctor told us Glenn has asthma. That's why she coughs so much."

"That doctor was wrong," said Dr. Martin. "Glenn has a serious disease, and it won't go away."

Glenn said, "I know a kid at school with cystic fibrosis, and he coughs all the time. Sometimes he spits up stuff. He misses a lot of school. I heard someone say he won't live another year. Will I die soon?"

Did You Know?

The name *cystic fibrosis* describes how the disease affects the pancreas. The disorder causes fibrosis. That means tissue in the pancreas becomes scarred and damaged. Healthy tissue also is replaced by cysts, or small holes filled with fluids.

Cystic fibrosis also is called mucoviscidosis. This means the body produces thick and sticky mucus in the lungs and digestive system.

The doctor's diagnosis, or determination, scared Glenn and her mother. Cystic fibrosis, or CF, is often a deadly disease. About one-half of all people with cystic fibrosis live to age 30. Some people live much longer. However, others with cystic fibrosis live only for a few years or months.

Cystic fibrosis affects tens of thousands of people worldwide. In the United States, it is the most common fatal genetic disease. A genetic disease is inherited, or passed on from parents to their children. About 2,500 babies are born with cystic fibrosis each year in the United States. In most cases, cystic fibrosis is diagnosed by the age of 3. Sometimes the disease isn't uncovered until the teen or early adult years.

Cystic fibrosis is chronic. The disease lasts a lifetime and usually gets worse over time. In the United States, 30,000 children and adults have cystic fibrosis. About 3,000 people in Canada and 20,000 Europeans have cystic fibrosis, too.

Bacteria, viruses, chemicals, and radiation do not cause cystic fibrosis. This disorder isn't spread from person to person like a cold or the flu. It is safe to be near people with cystic fibrosis.

Cystic Fibrosis

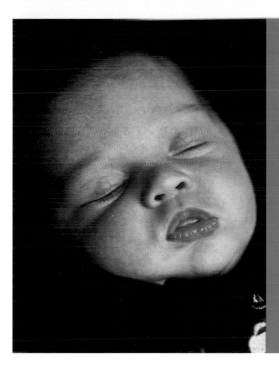

Cystic fibrosis is the result of an abnormal gene that people have when they are born.

A Genetic Disorder

Cystic fibrosis is a genetic disease. People with a genetic disease such as CF are born with it and cannot outgrow it. Instead, these people must live with the disease throughout their life.

People who have CF get a defective gene from each parent. The defective gene produces an abnormal, or unusual, form of the protein called CFTR. This protein changes the way chloride moves in and out of cells. Chloride is a part of salt, or sodium chloride.

The change in chloride's movement affects the balance of salt and water in the body. A proper balance of salt and water keeps mucus thin and slippery. Mucus lines the lungs and pancreas as well as passages to other body organs. The pancreas is an organ that helps break down food. The change cystic fibrosis causes in the movement of chloride results in thick, sticky mucus.

Glenn Wonders Why

Glenn wondered what she had done to cause her cystic fibrosis.

"Dr. Martin, how did I get this disease? I don't smoke or drink alcohol. I don't do any drugs. I get pretty good grades and like to skate and play softball."

Dr. Martin said, "Glenn, you aren't being punished for something you've done. You haven't done anything wrong. It sounds like you take good care of yourself. You need to keep doing that."

Who Gets Cystic Fibrosis?

A child must inherit two cystic fibrosis genes—one from each parent—to have the disease. Each person receives two sets of genes. One set comes from the mother and one set comes from the father. A baby will not develop cystic fibrosis if he or she inherits only one cystic fibrosis gene. If both parents have a CF gene, each child they have has a 25 percent risk of having CF.

About 1 in every 20 to 25 Americans is a carrier of cystic fibrosis. Carriers each have one cystic fibrosis gene. These people seldom know they are carriers because they have no symptoms, or signs, of the disease. The chance of being a cystic fibrosis carrier increases if family members have cystic fibrosis or are carriers.

Humans have 23 pairs of chromosomes. These are made of molecules called DNA that carry the genetic code. In 1989, researchers discovered the location of the gene that, when defective, causes cystic fibrosis. This gene is found on chromosome number 7. More than 800 different kinds of CF genes have been identified so far.

Cystic fibrosis occurs equally in both males and females. CF can affect all races and ethnic groups. However, this disease strikes mostly Caucasians whose ancestors come from northern Europe. CF is much less common in Latinos and African Americans and even rarer in American Indians and Asian Americans.

Systems Affected

The lungs and respiratory system are hit the hardest in most people with CF. These people may cough a lot and have trouble breathing. They also may get lung infections easily.

In many people with CF, the digestive system is affected. The small intestine doesn't fully digest food. Therefore, with cystic fibrosis, people cannot get much nutrition from what they eat and drink. That means they don't get many of the substances needed for good health, which foods provide.

Cystic fibrosis affects the sweat glands, too. People with cystic fibrosis lose a lot of salt when they sweat. Loss of too much salt can occur during exercise, with a high fever, or in hot weather.

In males especially, CF can affect the reproductive system. That means that without special surgery, many males with CF cannot have children.

As far back as the 1600s, doctors described children who probably had cystic fibrosis.

The Mystery of Cystic Fibrosis

For many years, doctors didn't understand that cystic fibrosis affected so many body systems. In the 1930s, health experts began to wonder if they were seeing a new disease. Doctors had long recognized that some infants couldn't digest their food well. These babies didn't grow as fast as other babies. Other doctors saw children cough a lot or develop ongoing lung infections. Many of these young people died at an early age.

For centuries, doctors didn't realize that these symptoms were all part of the same disease. That's because all these symptoms were common to other diseases.

In 1938, Dr. Dorothy H. Andersen first reported cystic fibrosis as a separate disease. Dr. Andersen and her team of doctors studied the medical history of children with unusual digestive and lung problems. The doctors found that the pancreas, lungs, and other body organs of these children were damaged and infected. Dr. Andersen named the new disease *cystic fibrosis of the pancreas*. Dr. Andersen continued to study cystic fibrosis. In 1946, she became the first doctor to recommend a special diet for people with CF.

There are many kinds of inherited health disorders. Some occur among certain cultural groups. Inherited diseases include:

- Color blindness: This condition means that a person cannot see one or more colors.

  - Hemophilia: This is a disorder in which a person's blood doesn't clot. The person bleeds too much even from small cuts.

    - Sickle-cell anemia: This blood disease is caused by abnormal red blood cells. (It most often affects people of African, Mediterranean, or Southwest Asian ancestry.)

      - Tay-Sachs disease: This disease destroys the nervous system. (It most often affects people of eastern European Jewish ancestry.)

A heat wave in New York City in 1952 helped doctors find another clue to the mystery of cystic fibrosis. It had long been known that some children had very salty skin. Doctors did not yet know that this was another common symptom of CF. During the heat wave, many children with CF were rushed to local hospitals. These children were weak and dehydrated, which means they needed lots of fluids fast. From this crisis, doctors realized that people with CF often have high salt levels in their sweat.

Points to Consider

What did you know about cystic fibrosis before reading this chapter?

What information would you be able to give to someone who didn't know much about cystic fibrosis?

Do you know anyone who has cystic fibrosis? Are there students in your school with cystic fibrosis?

Would you treat someone with CF differently than someone without CF? Why or why not?

Chapter Overview

When people have cystic fibrosis, the cells lining the respiratory system produce thick mucus that blocks the airways and lungs. As a result, breathing problems, lung infections, and lung damage often occur.

Most people with cystic fibrosis develop problems with the digestive system. These people often do not have enough enzymes for normal food digestion.

The sweat glands do not work correctly in people with cystic fibrosis. They usually have too much salt in their sweat.

Most males with cystic fibrosis are sterile. Unless they have special surgery, they cannot get a female pregnant. Some females have difficulty getting pregnant because of problems from their cystic fibrosis. If they do become pregnant, they may have problems with their pregnancy.

Chapter 2

How Cystic Fibrosis Affects the Body

Cystic fibrosis affects four main body systems. These are the respiratory system, the digestive system, the sweat glands, and the reproductive system.

Respiratory Problems

Respiratory problems are the most serious symptoms of cystic fibrosis. Knowing about the respiratory system can help to understand the effect CF has on it.

The Respiratory System

The lungs are part of the respiratory system. Inhaling, or breathing in, brings oxygen to the bloodstream. Exhaling, or breathing out, releases a waste gas from the blood. This gas is called carbon dioxide.

Some people with cystic fibrosis develop diabetes. In this disease, the body cannot use the sugars and starches in food for energy. Diabetes results when the pancreas doesn't produce enough insulin. This hormone maintains the correct level of certain chemicals in the blood. When someone has diabetes, these chemicals can build up and cause blindness, heart disease, or kidney problems.

Normally, air enters the body through the nose or mouth. It travels through the larynx (voice box) and enters the trachea (windpipe). The windpipe divides into two main branches, called bronchial tubes. One branch goes into the left lung. The other goes into the right lung. In the lungs, the bronchial tubes divide into smaller tubes, or bronchioles, that deliver oxygen throughout the lungs.

The cells lining the respiratory tract, or system, normally produce a thin layer of mucus. This substance coats the inner walls of the airways. It helps to clean the air and protect the airways.

Dave, Age 12

Dave has a moderate case of cystic fibrosis. Dave looked healthy when he was born. His parents were thrilled to take their new son home from the hospital. One month later, Dave started to choke and his face turned blue. His father tried to help him breathe, but nothing worked. Then his father smacked Dave on the back. A wad of dark mucus shot out of Dave's mouth, and the baby started to cry. Dave's parents rushed him to the hospital. Once there, the doctor checked Dave carefully.

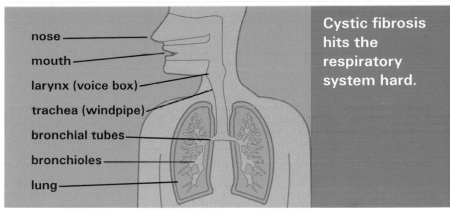

nose
mouth
larynx (voice box)
trachea (windpipe)
bronchial tubes
bronchioles
lung

Cystic fibrosis hits the respiratory system hard.

Cystic Fibrosis and the Respiratory System

A main symptom of cystic fibrosis is thick and sticky mucus that clogs many bronchioles in the lungs. As a result, parts of the lungs become blocked off by mucus. Air gets trapped in some of the small tubes. Then the lungs don't work well. The person may cough or wheeze a lot and have difficulty breathing. This loss of lung ability also results in another problem. When not used, parts of the lung can become weak and diseased, and they can even collapse. Lung disease usually is the eventual cause of death in most people with cystic fibrosis.

Ongoing lung problems often lead to lung infections. The bronchial tubes can become infected and swollen. This can result in bronchitis, or inflamed bronchial tubes. People cough a lot with this painful disease. The small air passages also can become weak and lose the ability to perform their job. This can develop into a lung disease called bronchiectasis. People with bronchiectasis have great difficulty breathing and can have bleeding in their lungs.

Thick mucus makes it hard for the respiratory system to clear away dust and germs. That means bacteria can get trapped in the clogged tubes. As bacteria multiply, they can cause infections in the lungs. As a result, people with cystic fibrosis often develop bacterial infections. Sometimes they get infections from fungi. Both types of infections can be deadly if not treated effectively or correctly.

Sweat glands are found in most areas of the body. Two places have the most sweat glands: the bottom of the feet and the palm of the hands. Each person has about 2 million sweat glands.

Digestive System

Most people with cystic fibrosis develop problems with their digestive system. The thick mucus clogs the pancreas. This blocks enzymes that are made in the pancreas from moving to the intestines. Enzymes break down food that supplies the body with nutrients, or healthy substances.

Most people with CF do not have enough enzymes for normal digestion of fatty foods. These people tend to pass a lot of undigested food out of the body. Without good digestion, the body grows and develops slowly. Without treatment, people with CF lose weight and get weaker. Their body doesn't handle infections as well as the body of people with CF who get good nutrition.

Sweat Glands

The sweat glands help keep body temperature normal. Everyone sweats all the time. This is true whether it's winter or summer or whether people are asleep or awake. People usually sweat more when they're hot or under stress. The extra sweat helps them cool down. The sweat glands remove some body wastes such as salt as well.

When people have CF, the sweat glands don't work correctly. These people lose too much salt through their sweat. They have two to five times the normal amount of salt in their sweat. Not having enough salt in the body can cause problems, including tiredness, weakness, fever, muscle cramps, and stomach pain. Some people vomit, or throw up. Dehydration can occur, leaving people without enough water for their body to work properly.

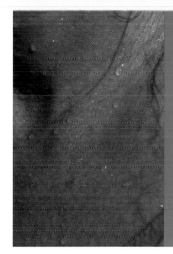

People with cystic fibrosis usually have very salty sweat because their sweat glands don't work properly.

The balance of minerals in the blood also can be affected when the sweat glands don't work normally. This can lead to irregular heart rhythms, fainting, or shock. During shock, blood pressure drops and all body systems slow down. The end result could be death.

Reproductive System

Almost all males with cystic fibrosis are sterile and cannot make a female pregnant. Males with cystic fibrosis still produce normal sperm. However, the tubes that transport these male sex cells to the testes usually do not develop. The testes are one of the male sex organs. There is a special surgery that can permit males with CF to father children.

Many females with cystic fibrosis can give birth. However, they may find it hard to get pregnant and to remain pregnant. Other women with cystic fibrosis cannot get pregnant. For them, their thick mucus totally blocks sperm from reaching the egg.

Cystic fibrosis doesn't affect the sex hormones. Both males and females with cystic fibrosis usually produce normal amounts. Yet teens with cystic fibrosis tend to develop sexually slower. This often is because of the nutritional problems that are common in cystic fibrosis.

A female with cystic fibrosis may have a difficult time becoming pregnant. If she does get pregnant, she may have trouble maintaining the pregnancy.

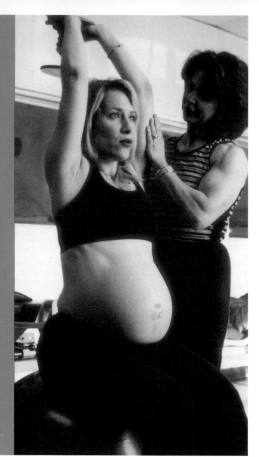

"I was diagnosed with cystic fibrosis at age 3. I have two brothers and two sisters. I loved having so many brothers and sisters in my family. There was always someone to play with and to listen to my problems. I married Darren last year, and we decided we wanted to start a family right away.

Tami, Age 23

"My doctor was worried when I told her that we wanted a baby. She said getting pregnant could strain my body and make my lungs worse. She also said I could have trouble getting pregnant, that it wasn't easy for some women with cystic fibrosis. I was lucky and got pregnant. So far, my pregnancy has been going okay. I do get tired fast and need to rest often."

Some people with cystic fibrosis have an unusual curve of the spine. This condition is called kyphosis and happens in about one out of four people with cystic fibrosis. Kyphosis can cause a person's chest to look barrel-shaped.

Points to Consider

How would you react to someone who had difficulty breathing? Why do you think you would react this way?

Why is it important for someone with cystic fibrosis to avoid someone with a cold or other infectious disease?

In what way is cystic fibrosis like a time bomb?

Why could a male with cystic fibrosis have a false sense of security about practicing unsafe sex?

Chapter Overview

Some children with cystic fibrosis show symptoms in infancy. Others don't show symptoms until they're older.

Salty-tasting skin, frequent lung infections, breathing difficulties, and lack of healthy weight gain are the main signs of CF.

Diagnosing cystic fibrosis can be difficult at times. Its symptoms are similar to those of many other diseases. Early detection of cystic fibrosis can lead to early treatment. This means the child will have a better chance to grow and develop.

Diagnosing cystic fibrosis involves several steps. These include a medical history, a physical examination, and various tests. Two tests are the most important in diagnosing cystic fibrosis. One is the sweat test, and the other is the blood test for the CF gene.

Chapter 3

Diagnosing Cystic Fibrosis

Delfin and Karan happily
announced the birth of their first

child, Casey. But right from the start, something was wrong.
Casey seemed to struggle for every breath. His diapers hung on
his skinny legs, and he had constant lung infections. At 6
months, Casey had gained just a few pounds over his birth
weight. Delfin and Karan were frightened and worried. What
was wrong with their baby?

The Symptoms of Cystic Fibrosis

Delfin and Karan's baby showed symptoms of cystic fibrosis.
Some children with cystic fibrosis have no obvious symptoms
except a chronic cough until they're toddlers or teens. Other
children, like Casey, show serious symptoms soon after birth.

One of the signs of cystic fibrosis is frequent sinus infections.

There are four main symptoms of cystic fibrosis. People with cystic fibrosis have some or all of them.

Salty-tasting skin

Ongoing coughing, wheezing, or frequent lung infections such as pneumonia

Loose, foul-smelling stools (solid body waste)

Poor weight gain, even when eating a lot

There are other various but important signs of cystic fibrosis. A baby or adult with cystic fibrosis may have one, some, or all of these:

Frequent sinus infections; sinuses are the open cavities in the nose and face.

Lack of energy

Smaller height and weight than average

Frequent dehydration and exhaustion in hot weather

Finger clubbing (Tips of fingers and toes become larger than normal and may be more rounded.)

Nasal polyps, or masses inside the nose

Cystic fibrosis symptoms vary from person to person. Symptoms may appear suddenly only once in a while, or they may occur regularly. Sometimes, signs of the disease do not appear until the person becomes a teen or an adult.

Cystic fibrosis has other signs, too. People with CF may be tense or irritable because of discomfort. They may dislike playing sports or doing much physical activity because they get winded easily. People with CF may sound congested or have a nasal voice. They may avoid going places where they must climb many stairs or walk long distances.

Difficulties in Diagnosis

Diagnosing cystic fibrosis can be difficult. In CF's early stage, a child often seems healthy and has a good appetite. After some time passes, the child may not gain much or any weight. Parents may notice that the child gets one cold after another. However, these early signs are the same as those of many other health problems. For example, these same symptoms could point to asthma or digestive problems.

In general, a baby born with cystic fibrosis usually has symptoms during the first year. Sometimes cystic fibrosis symptoms are mild while a child is young. The symptoms may not become more serious until the teen years. Therefore, some people with CF may go until their teen or adult years before being diagnosed.

Diagnosing cystic fibrosis as early as possible is important. The earlier cystic fibrosis is detected, the earlier treatment can begin. Early treatment means a child with CF has a better chance to grow and develop.

At a
Glance

Before 1900, people in northern Europe had a saying. "Woe to that child which when kissed on the forehead tastes salty. He is bewitched and soon must die." People did not realize that this referred to children with cystic fibrosis.

Steps in Diagnosis

Diagnosing cystic fibrosis involves several steps. Doctors first take the person's medical history. They want to know about the person's past health. They also want to know about serious illnesses among family members. This information might help to explain the person's symptoms.

The next step is a physical exam. Doctors observe the person's general health. They check blood pressure, temperature, and heart rate. In addition, they listen to the person's breathing and breathing muscles. They also examine the eyes, ears, nose, and throat for signs of infection.

Laboratory tests are an important part of diagnosing CF. The most common test for cystic fibrosis is the sweat test. It measures the amount of salt, or sodium chloride, in a person's sweat.

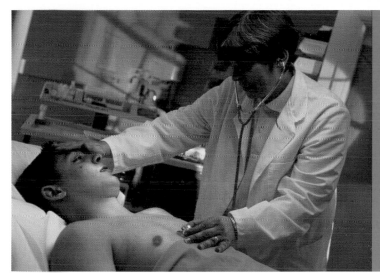

Listening to a person's breathing and breathing muscles is one part of diagnosing cystic fibrosis.

Jeffrey, Age 15

"When I was 12, I was tested for cystic fibrosis with a sweat test. My doctor explained each step. First, she placed electrodes on my forearm. These electrical devices produce a weak electric current. Then she put a thin pad over the electrodes to absorb my sweat. The pad was soaked with a drug called pilocarpine, a harmless drug that promotes sweating. Finally, she wrapped the whole area in plastic.

"When everything was ready, the doctor sent a very small amount of electricity through the electrodes. This electric current drove the pilocarpine into my skin. The drug made my sweat glands produce sweat. I didn't feel any pain when I got zapped.

"After that, the doctor removed everything and covered the area with a piece of filter paper. The filter paper collected my sweat for 30 minutes. I had to sit quietly, no wiggling or stretching. The doctor removed the filter paper and sent it to the lab. The lab people then analyzed the amount of chloride in my sweat."

Fast Fact

A small percentage of people with cystic fibrosis have normal sweat chloride levels. The sweat test doesn't work on them, so they must be diagnosed by gene testing.

Other tests doctors might use in diagnosing cystic fibrosis include:

Gene tests. A sample of blood or cells scraped from the inside of the cheek can be checked for the cystic fibrosis gene. A doctor can tell if someone has cystic fibrosis by analyzing the genes.

Chest X rays. These can tell the doctor if cystic fibrosis has damaged the lungs and other air passages.

Pulmonary function tests. These tests measure how well the lungs are working. They also tell how well the lungs respond to treatment.

Pancreas tests. These tests involve a sample of blood or urine, which is liquid body waste. The sample is tested for normal amounts of certain substances that come from the pancreas. If the amounts are low, this can indicate cystic fibrosis.

Sputum tests. Sputum is mucus coughed up from the lungs. Studying a sample of sputum might show bacteria related to cystic fibrosis. Or, it might show substances from other diseases such as asthma.

Cystic Fibrosis

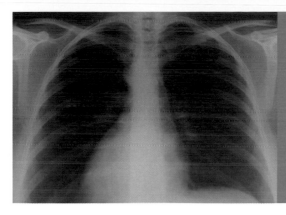

A chest X ray is one test a doctor might use to determine whether a person has cystic fibrosis.

After the Diagnosis, Jeffrey's Experience

The sweat test confirmed that Jeffrey had cystic fibrosis. Jeffrey had two times the normal amount of chloride in his sweat. The sweat test only shows if a person has cystic fibrosis. The amount of chloride in the sweat doesn't tell the doctor anything about the severity of the disease. The test results can't be used to predict if a person will develop a mild or severe form of cystic fibrosis.

Jeffrey and his parents were surprised when they heard the diagnosis. No one in their family had cystic fibrosis or any other genetic diseases. The doctor referred Jeffrey to a special cystic fibrosis clinic for treatment.

Points to Consider

Do you know your family's medical history? If not, how can you find this information?

Has anyone in your family ever been diagnosed with a serious illness? How did you react? If not, how do you think you would react?

Describe a time you were sick and didn't know what you had. What were your symptoms? What steps did the doctor take to diagnose your illness?

How do you think you would feel if you found out you had CF?

Chapter Overview

Cystic fibrosis cannot be cured, but it can be treated so that people can lead a fairly normal life. Treatment varies depending on how far the disease has progressed and which body systems are affected.

Lung treatments work to clear the lungs and make breathing easier. Various drugs can be inhaled to help thin and loosen mucus in the lungs. Chest physical therapy and regular exercise also help loosen mucus.

Other treatments for CF focus on reducing digestive problems. People with cystic fibrosis usually follow a special diet. They also take enzyme supplements and vitamins.

Lung transplants are a last resort for some people with cystic fibrosis.

Many skilled professionals can help people with cystic fibrosis. Family and friends can provide important support and care, too.

Chapter 4

Managing Cystic Fibrosis

Cystic fibrosis has no cure, but various treatments can help to improve breathing and digestive problems. The goal of treatment is to avoid lung and other body system damage. This slows the progress of the disease and helps the person lead a normal life.

Treatment for cystic fibrosis is not simple because each person is different. Doctors design a treatment plan to fit each person's needs. They consider the person's age, symptoms, and general health. They also consider the severity of the disease and what body systems are affected.

Family members can give chest physical therapy (CPT) to a child with cystic fibrosis. Teens and adults can learn to do CPT by themselves. Electric chest clappers and vibrators can help teens perform their own CPT.

Lung Treatment

Most CF treatment focuses on clearing the lungs of the thick mucus that clogs the airways. Without treatment, people with cystic fibrosis have difficulty breathing and develop chronic lung infections.

To fight these problems, lung treatment loosens and thins out the thick mucus in the airways. Treatment also works to keep the lungs working well. Various treatment methods include medicines and physical therapy.

Medicines

Several types of drugs are used routinely by people with CF.

Antibiotics. These are medicines that fight off infections. Antibiotics can be taken by mouth as a pill or liquid or inhaled as a mist. Some people need regular hospital visits to get intravenous, or IV, antibiotics. With this method, antibiotics are put directly into the veins.

Decongestants. These drugs shrink the small blood vessels in the nose. This reduces pressure in the nasal passages, which usually helps the person to breathe more easily.

Bronchodilators. These drugs widen the breathing tubes to make breathing easier.

Mucolytics. These drugs thin mucus, which makes it easier for mucus to drain out of the lungs.

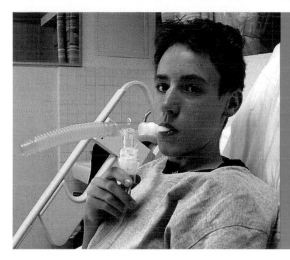

People with cystic fibrosis sometimes use a nebulizer to inhale their medication.

Decongestants, bronchodilators, certain antibiotics, and mucolytics can be taken as pills or liquids. Many people with CF inhale these drugs by using a nebulizer. This machine turns liquid medicines into a mist. People breathe in the mist for about 15 to 20 minutes. The mist goes deep into the lungs. Nebulizers are too big to carry around and must be used at home.

Chest Physical Therapy

A treatment called chest physical therapy, or CPT, often is needed one to three times a day. During CPT, the person with CF sits or lies so that mucus drains toward the throat. Another person gently and rapidly claps or thumps the person's chest or back with cupped hands. This helps to dislodge the mucus from the airways. The thick mucus moves up to the throat and then is coughed up and spit into a cup. The clapping is done on about 12 areas of the chest and back. CPT takes about 30 minutes to do. Some people with CF use special machines to help them get rid of the thick mucus.

Exercise

Exercise is an important part of cystic fibrosis treatment. Exercise can greatly improve the breathing muscles and strengthen the heart. It can help loosen mucus in the lungs. Exercise also helps the person cough to clear the mucus.

A well-planned exercise program can be important for a person with cystic fibrosis. Gardening is an example of easy exercise that can be part of such a program.

An exercise program should be well planned and supervised. People with CF usually are encouraged to choose exercises they enjoy. Popular exercises include swimming, biking, running, weight training, and bouncing on a trampoline. Playing sports is another way to get exercise. Basketball, softball, tennis, skiing, skating, and soccer are some good examples. Less vigorous exercise such as walking or gardening is good, too. People with CF may need to get extra fluids and salt when they exercise.

Sara, Age 16

Sara's cystic fibrosis has never gotten in the way of her sports and activities. She played volleyball and was a member of the dance line at her junior high school. Now, Sara has taken up running and cross-country skiing. Running and skiing are more than just sports for Sara. "When I don't practice for a few days, I can feel the difference. My lungs don't seem clear."

Along with exercise, Sara takes medicines three times a day for her cystic fibrosis. Every night, she wears a vibrating vest for one hour. This loosens the mucus in her lungs. Sara goes to a hospital for exams every three months.

Cystic Fibrosis

Digestive Treatment

Without treatment, many people with cystic fibrosis cannot digest food properly. Three types of treatment help digestive problems: diet, enzyme supplements, and vitamins.

Some people with CF may need to eat a high-calorie, high-protein, high-fat diet because some nutrients aren't absorbed properly. The extra food keeps the body healthy and helps the body grow. A healthy body can better fight off infections. The following chart lists ways people with cystic fibrosis can add calories to their diet.

Some Ways to Add Calories to the Diet

Add cheese to scrambled eggs, casseroles, and sandwiches.

Spread butter on bread for sandwiches.

Put grated Parmesan cheese on pasta, casseroles, popcorn, and salads.

Have gravy on foods such as meat, potatoes, rice, noodles, and French fries.

Add chopped nuts to cookie and bread dough and pancake batter.

Most (if not all) people with CF take supplements of pancreatic enzymes. These enzymes go from the stomach into the small intestine. There, they help break down food into nutrients that the body can use.

People with cystic fibrosis often need to get more calories than other people do.

Most people with cystic fibrosis take two multivitamins each day. In addition, they may need to add salt to their diet. This helps to replace the salt lost in their sweat.

"I need to eat more food and calories than other kids. That's because the thick mucus from my cystic fibrosis prevents some foods from being digested and absorbed. I need a lot of proteins, which help to keep my body strong. So I eat a lot of dairy foods such as milk, cheese, and ice cream. My friends giggle when I spread lots of butter on my sandwiches and veggies.

Lynn, Age 14

"I also need to eat more fats than other people do. That's because fats provide more calories per ounce than proteins or carbohydrates do. So I eat rich cheese sauces, creamy soups, and pour gravy on my mashed potatoes. I also eat nuts by the handful. My diet isn't at all what usually is considered healthy. But it's what I need to stay healthy. So I enjoy my friends' groans and moans when I eat more pizza than any of them!"

Lung Transplants

A lung transplant is the last resort for some people with cystic fibrosis. In a transplant operation, people with cystic fibrosis get new lungs if their own become too diseased. Usually, a transplant is considered only when a person's disease is advanced or if standard treatments don't work well. Lung transplants are a major breakthrough in treating cystic fibrosis.

The Management Team

Many children and teens need various people to help manage their cystic fibrosis. The team may include doctors, nurses, therapists, teachers, social workers, a pharmacist, and a dietitian. A pharmacist is trained to prepare and sell medicines. A dietitian is a nutrition specialist.

Family members are an important part of the team, too. They can provide love and encouragement. They can help with therapy and medications at home, go along on doctor's appointments, and provide financial support.

As the child becomes older, he or she can become an active part of the management team. It's important for teens with CF to be involved in decisions about their health care.

Points to Consider

Why might it be hard for a teen with cystic fibrosis to stick to a treatment program?

Why is it important that people with cystic fibrosis tell their doctor about any drug they take or plan to take?

Imagine that you need to have therapy for an hour or more every day. How would this change your daily life?

Juan avoids all exercise because he has cystic fibrosis. Is he managing his disease well? Why or why not?

How could you be part of the management team for a friend with cystic fibrosis?

Chapter Overview

People with cystic fibrosis and their family often experience high levels of stress. The support of other people can help them cope.

Many sources of support are available for people with cystic fibrosis and their family. These sources include health care professionals, mental health counselors, social workers, and organizations that help people with cystic fibrosis. Other people with cystic fibrosis as well as friends and relatives also can provide support.

Support can take many forms. It can be information, financial aid, or counseling. It can be a willingness to listen and a shoulder to cry on. Practical help such as running errands or doing chores also are forms of support.

Chapter 5

Finding Support

People with CF and their family often experience high levels of stress. The ongoing care of a seriously ill family member can be exhausting. Sometimes, it's difficult to keep up with school, jobs, and other responsibilities. There are many things to worry about, such as the future and the high cost of medical treatment. Fortunately, people and groups are available to lend support to those with CF and their family.

Health Care Professionals

Many health care professionals are involved in caring for a person with CF. These professionals work as a team. Each contributes special knowledge and skills. Having a team of experts on hand can lessen a family's anxiety.

Doctors are only one part of a person's cystic fibrosis management team.

Doctors

People with CF usually have several doctors. One of the doctors coordinates care. This doctor provides treatment and support by explaining treatment options and answering questions. Another responsibility of this doctor is to work with the other health care professionals on the management team.

Open and honest conversations with the doctors can help. People with cystic fibrosis need to let their doctor know about their physical well-being, moods, and any problems. This helps the doctor plan treatment and make the right changes to plans.

Nurses

People with cystic fibrosis often spend days, weeks, or even months in the hospital. As a result, they often have more contact with nurses than any other health care professionals. Nurses take care of physical needs and also provide emotional support. They listen to people's worries and can understand what they are going through. Nurses often are the first to recognize and alert other team members to changes in the person's medical condition.

Dietitians

No diet can cure cystic fibrosis. However, good nutrition is important for getting better and staying strong. Dietitians help plan a suitable diet with enough calories for people with cystic fibrosis.

Cystic Fibrosis

Respiratory Therapists

Respiratory therapists help keep the airways clear for people with CF. These therapists provide direct care to people with cystic fibrosis. They also teach family members how to do CPT and to give the nebulizer (mist medications) correctly.

Other Hospital Staff

A stay in a hospital can be stressful. To reduce stress, patient-care coordinators help answer questions and resolve problems. They can help communicate a person's needs to the hospital staff. Discharge planners help arrange for the care of the person after leaving the hospital.

Mental Health Counselors

A serious illness affects the emotions as well as the body. It's normal for people with cystic fibrosis to feel angry, sad, anxious, and frightened. Mental health professionals such as psychologists and psychiatrists can help these people and their family deal with these feelings. Many people find comfort talking with spiritual leaders such as rabbis, priests, or ministers.

Social Workers

Social workers also help maintain the emotional health of people with cystic fibrosis and their family. After the diagnosis, the social worker evaluates the family's ability to cope and provides support when needed. For example, families can get individual or group counseling from social workers. Social workers can arrange help from government programs. Such help might include financial aid for medicines, transportation, equipment, or short-term housing.

The Cystic Fibrosis Foundation was established in 1955. It's the largest cystic fibrosis organization in the United States. The foundation has two goals. One is to assure the development of ways to cure and control cystic fibrosis. The other goal is to improve the quality of life for people with the disease. The Cystic Fibrosis Foundation supports more than 110 cystic fibrosis care centers in the United States. These centers are located at large hospitals and provide high-quality, specialized care for people with cystic fibrosis. Doctors at the centers offer diagnosis and treatment.

Social workers help prepare young people for independent living by providing guidance in education, career choices, and family planning. These professionals can help with marriage problems or conflicts between parents and children.

Organizations

Several organizations exist to assist people with CF and their family. These organizations also support cystic fibrosis research. They include the Cystic Fibrosis Foundation (CFF), Cystic Fibrosis Research, Inc. (CFRI), International Association of Cystic Fibrosis Adults (IACFA), and Canadian Cystic Fibrosis Foundation (CCFF). You can find contact information for these organizations at the back of this book. Here are some of the services these groups provide:

Free information about cystic fibrosis and treatment methods

Support groups for children and teens with cystic fibrosis, their parents, and their brothers and sisters

Financial help or assistance finding sources of financial aid

Referrals to cystic fibrosis specialists

Counseling

Getting to know others who have cystic fibrosis can be a good way to find emotional support.

Other People With Cystic Fibrosis

Other people with cystic fibrosis can be a source of emotional support. People with cystic fibrosis often share a special bond. They know what having the disease is like. They can talk about things they may not want to talk about with their family. Many people with cystic fibrosis have a bright outlook. They are determined to lead a normal, happy life. These people can be role models for others. A doctor or nearby hospital can help people with cystic fibrosis find local support groups.

Brandon, Age 15

"I used to dread going to the hospital for my cystic fibrosis treatments. Sometimes I'd need to stay for weeks. Then I decided to help others like myself. I thought that if I stopped thinking about my problems, I'd feel better.

"This works! Now when I'm at the hospital, I try to make new friends, especially with other teens and younger kids. I ask the nurses in the hospital for fun stickers, games, and videos. Then I invite kids to my room or organize a place where we can be together. What's even better is that my family and friends come to visit me more often when my spirits are up. I never realized I could provide support for others, even when I'm in the hospital."

If teens and their family can't afford to get medical treatment, they can try various resources, such as:

- Talking with the school nurse. Teens and their family can ask for a referral to a local clinic or health care center.
- Calling a local or county health clinic
- Calling a local hospital and asking what free services are available
- Calling the state public assistance office
- Calling the local public health office
- Calling a local social services office. In many states, people can apply for benefits at local and state welfare, public health, or social service agencies.

Friends and Relatives

Friends and relatives can provide emotional and practical support. Emotional support can include visits, telephone calls, and cards. Giving a hug or a pat on the shoulder can let people with CF know they're not alone. Sending or bringing over flowers or a plant can show care and support.

You can offer practical support in many ways. Friends and relatives might prepare a meal for the family or run errands. They might do household chores, bring over favorite foods, or provide transportation to doctor appointments.

Most friends and relatives want to help, but sometimes they don't know what to do. In that case, they need to ask how to help. Also, it's okay for people with cystic fibrosis or their family to let their needs be known. They can ask for help with simple chores or homework, for example.

Friends and family may be able to do simple tasks to help out a loved one who has cystic fibrosis.

Friends and relatives may not know what to say about the person's illness. People with cystic fibrosis can take the lead here. They can say, "I do (I don't) want to talk about it." Or they can say that they want to talk about something that is bothering them. It's best to be open and honest. This helps prevent fear and misunderstanding.

Points to Consider

What help might your family need if a family member became seriously ill? Whom could you count on?

How might your life change if you had to be in the hospital for extended periods of time?

Make a list of practical things you could do to help a neighbor or friend who is dealing with a medical crisis.

Chapter Overview

Cystic fibrosis is hard to deal with at any age. It presents special challenges for teens. Cystic fibrosis may slow a teen's physical development.

Males with CF often are sterile, and females often have a hard time getting pregnant. However, practicing safe and responsible sex is important for any sexually active teen.

Cystic fibrosis can interfere with a teen's desire to fit in. It can hinder school activities. It can affect relationships with friends, parents, and other family members.

An important way for teens with cystic fibrosis to cope is to follow their treatment plan. When the disease is under control, many teens can lead an active, healthy life.

Dealing with cystic fibrosis can have a positive side. Teens can learn about self-discipline. They can learn to handle life with humor and a positive attitude.

Chapter 6

Living With Cystic Fibrosis

Living with a chronic illness such as cystic fibrosis can be difficult. It may be especially difficult for teens. That's because teens are already dealing with the hard task of growing up. Dealing with cystic fibrosis along with everything else can be a lot to handle. In addition, teens experience physical changes during puberty. That's when the body changes from a child's to an adult's. These physical changes can make a teen's cystic fibrosis harder to control.

"I'm different from most other kids. I cough a lot and have to watch what I eat. I take a lot of medicines. Some people may think I'm odd. My mom told me that having cystic fibrosis is like having blue hair or yellow eyes. It doesn't have anything to do with what's on the inside. I try to look beyond the surface of people and see what makes them different and interesting. I hope that's how others look at me."—Anna, age 14

Slower Physical Development

Teens with CF often are shorter and smaller than other teens. They may not develop as fast as their friends. Girls with cystic fibrosis tend to start developing sexually at age 15 to 17. That's when they start their period. Boys develop even later. They may not grow a beard or their voice may not deepen until age 16 or older.

It may seem like all other male teens are shaving or female teens are wearing bras. But all teens grow at their own pace. Some teens who don't have CF develop early, while others don't start until late in their teen years.

Sexuality

Practicing safe and responsible sex is important for all sexually active teens. Using a condom each time during sex helps to protect against sexually transmitted diseases. These are diseases that can be passed during sexual intercourse. Females with CF often have a harder time getting pregnant than other females do. However, they usually still can become pregnant.

Most males with cystic fibrosis are sterile. However, responsible males always should assume they can cause a pregnancy. Both male and female teens, if sexually active, need to protect themselves against unplanned pregnancy and disease.

Cystic Fibrosis

Boys with cystic fibrosis may develop sexually at a later age than most other boys do.

Fitting In

Most teens want to be like other teens. They may fear being different. Cystic fibrosis makes teens different. Some teens with CF cough a lot. Teens with CF often have trouble gaining weight. They tend to be smaller and thinner than average.

Also, teens with cystic fibrosis often take a lot of medicine and use inhalers. They usually need therapy each day. They must be on the outlook constantly for any changes in their health. Most have to stay in the hospital from time to time to get treatments.

"I have to go into the hospital once, sometimes twice, a year. That's when I get my 'tune-up.' It's kind of like taking a car to a garage to make sure everything is working all right. When I go to the hospital for my tune-up, I bring my favorite games, books, and jigsaw puzzles. That helps the time go faster. I also pack comfy clothes and tuck in a photo of my family."

Vera, Age 13

You may be able to help a friend with cystic fibrosis keep up with homework. For example, you could bring home his or her school assignments.

Missing School

Teens with cystic fibrosis may miss a lot of school. They may feel tired a lot. They may go to the doctor often. Therefore, they may find it difficult to keep up with homework.

To keep current with homework, teens can ask for special arrangements. Teens with CF should explain their situation to teachers and other school workers. Teachers can allow more time for assignments. Sometimes tutoring or homebound teaching is available. Teens with CF often can find someone in each class to take notes and carry home assignments.

Telling Others

Teens with cystic fibrosis may wonder when and what to tell others about their condition. Telling close friends is important. Knowing about the disease can help keep friends from getting scared and worried. Letting them know helps avoid uncomfortable situations for you and your friends. You won't have to worry about what they'll think if you cough a lot or take dozens of medicines in a restaurant.

Some friends may not be able to cope with your condition. They may love you but may be frightened of the future. So they may stop coming around. Hopefully, most friends will respond with care and understanding.

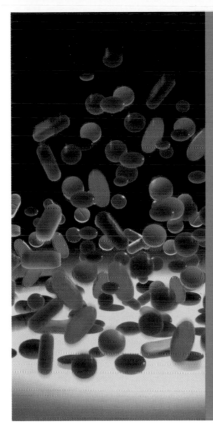

To stay healthy, a person with cystic fibrosis may take more than 25 pills, tablets, or capsules each day. These oral medicines typically include antibiotics, enzyme supplements, and vitamins.

Getting Along With Your Family

Cystic fibrosis affects a teen's family, including brothers and sisters. Parents may show special attention to the child with CF. Hospital visits, daily therapy, and special treatments may put the family in constant uproar. Brothers and sisters may come to resent the teen with cystic fibrosis.

Other times, brothers and sisters may worry about their sibling. They may be scared that he or she could die during a bad coughing fit or while in the hospital. They might feel guilty about being healthy.

Keeping a healthy home life can be challenging for families. Talking openly and honestly about problems and feelings helps. Often, counseling can be helpful in dealing with problems, too.

The Cystic Fibrosis Scholarship Foundation awards college scholarships to students with cystic fibrosis. For more information, contact the foundation at 2814 Grant Street, Evanston, IL 60201.

"My dad found out I had cystic fibrosis when I was 5. For a long time, he would fuss over me constantly. He wouldn't let me play softball or soccer. I couldn't do stuff with my friends, and I got teased for being a wimp. Finally, my dad went to an educational program. He talked with counselors and read lots of materials. He gave some to my brother and me to read.

"My dad learned to stop feeling guilty or responsible for causing my disease. He never knew he was a carrier. He couldn't have prevented it. My dad began treating me more like my brother and stopped trying to protect me so much. I joined a softball team this spring!"

Joe, Age 14

Becoming Independent

Overprotective parents can be a problem for many teens with a chronic illness. Like other teens, most teens with cystic fibrosis want to grow up and do things on their own. However, their parents may be afraid to let them try new things. They may worry about how their teen will manage without them.

Teens with cystic fibrosis deal with overprotective parents in different ways. One teen got his mother to join a support group. Now his mother discusses her concerns with other parents of teens with cystic fibrosis. Another teen arranged for friends to learn how to do chest therapy. Each friend takes a turn once or twice a week. This teen also learned how to do her own therapy with a vibrating vest.

Coping With Cystic Fibrosis

Living with cystic fibrosis is challenging. How the disease progresses is unknown. One month might be great, and the next month might mean a stay in the hospital. If you are a teen with CF, here are ways to help you cope:

Take your medicine and enzymes. Take your medicine as prescribed. Too little medicine may not help. Too much can be harmful. Tell your doctor about any side effects that trouble you. Your doctor may be able to prescribe a different medicine.

Follow your treatment plan. Sticking to your specific treatment plan can help you feel your best.

Be an active member of your health care team. Ask doctors and nurses questions about your disease. Keep track of your overall health and any specific problems. Write down this information. Then share your information with doctors, nurses, and others on your health care team. This information can help in planning and managing your treatment program.

Staying active is an important way to cope with cystic fibrosis.

Stay active. Keep your mind and body active. Exercise is important for people with cystic fibrosis. If you have concerns, talk with your doctor.

Join a support group for teens with CF. Don't have a local support group? Start one. Or, find a support group on the Internet. Through a support group, you can learn how other teens manage their cystic fibrosis. You can share problems and get advice.

Learn all you can about cystic fibrosis. Books, pamphlets, and videos are available. Some are for teens especially. Credible Internet sites also hold a wealth of information about CF.

Join an organization that works to improve life for people with cystic fibrosis. These organizations support cystic fibrosis research and education. They work for laws that guarantee the rights of people with CF. See pages 40 and 62 for a list of organizations.

Don't limit yourself. Do what you love to do, but avoid smoke and cigarettes.

- Cystic-L: Cystic Fibrosis Discussion and Support. Provides e-mail service and mailing list
  http://cystic-L.org

  - International Cystic Fibrosis Support Group. Provides contacts for those with an interest in cystic fibrosis
    http://cf.conncoll.edu

    - Support-Group.com. Provides links and bulletin boards for various diseases and illnesses, including cystic fibrosis
      www.support-group.com

      - Web of Care. Provides caregiver information specific to cystic fibrosis and has chat rooms and bulletin boards
        www.webofcare.com/cysticfibrosis.html

Dealing with CF can have positive effects. Teens may learn self-discipline. Coping with cystic fibrosis may help them learn to handle life with humor and a positive attitude.

Points to Consider

Describe a time when you were teased about something you had no control over. How did you feel? How did you react?

Why might brothers and sisters feel resentful of or angry toward a family member who has cystic fibrosis?

Why might the parents of a child with cystic fibrosis feel guilty? What types of behavior do you think the parents might display?

People you know are complaining about a teen who is coughing a lot. What could you do?

Chapter Overview

Advances in cystic fibrosis research and treatment have improved the survival rate for people with this disease. New forms of treatment promise to keep people with cystic fibrosis living a long, productive life.

Research continues along several avenues. These areas include gene therapy, drug treatment, and better therapy devices.

People with cystic fibrosis can participate in clinical trials. These studies help doctors find out if a new treatment is safe and effective.

Chapter 7

Looking Ahead

A diagnosis of cystic fibrosis was once a death sentence for a baby. This is no longer true. Many more people with CF are living a longer, fairly normal life. In 1955, children with CF often did not live past age 5. Since the 1990s, many people with CF live, on average, to age 32. Some now live into their 40s and 50s.

The improved life-expectancy rate reflects advances in the treatment of CF. These advances have come about through research. The following developments hold even more promise for people with CF. These developments may help people with CF to live a longer, more comfortable life.

Did You Know? The United States Congress approved $40 million to establish nine cystic fibrosis gene therapy centers. At these centers, scientists are developing gene therapy treatments.

Avenues for Research: Gene Therapy

Cystic fibrosis research is following several main avenues. One avenue is gene therapy, or genetic engineering. Researchers are developing ways to replace in cells the gene that causes cystic fibrosis with a normal one. Much of the research has focused on lung cells. Lung damage is the most common serious problem in cystic fibrosis. In some experiments, scientists have put normal genes into nose drops. A small number of people with cystic fibrosis have tried these nose drops. In some tests, the normal genes corrected small areas of the nasal passages for a short amount of time.

Researchers are looking for other ways to deliver replacement genes to the cells that need correcting. One way may be through adenovirus. This is the virus that causes the common cold. However, some people may be concerned about inhaling a virus. Another way to transport replacement genes may be fatty capsules called liposomes. Researchers also are considering the use of synthetic, or human-made, carriers.

Researchers have many questions about gene therapy. What is the best way to get normal genes into people with cystic fibrosis? What are the long-term results of this gene therapy? Can the salt problem be corrected? Finally, researchers wonder if gene therapy can one day cure or prevent lung disease in cystic fibrosis.

The first human cystic fibrosis gene therapy
experiments were performed in April 1993.

Fast
Fact

Avenues for Research: Drugs

A second avenue of research is to find new—or old—drugs to treat the disease. One promising drug is ibuprofen. This common pain reliever is available over-the-counter, or without a doctor's written order. Ibuprofen has helped reduce lung inflammation in children with CF. Inflammation is the process that causes fibrosis, or scarring. However, ibuprofen doesn't seem to help adults with CF. Studies are determining what amount of ibuprofen is best for children and if other current drugs could be useful. Drugs called macrolides are being tested in this area.

Bacterial infections in the lungs are a major problem in cystic fibrosis. Researchers have taken helpful IV antibiotic drugs and changed them to pills and aerosols, or sprays. These drug forms are easier to take and less costly than IV drugs. People can take them at home instead of having to go into the hospital. Other improved antibiotics are helping people with cystic fibrosis, too.

Researchers are working to find drugs that can correct the salt (chloride) problem in people with cystic fibrosis. They hope to create or find a drug that can help chloride move in and out of cells normally. This would balance the body's salt and water.

Protein repair therapy would help to fix the defective CFTR protein in people with cystic fibrosis. Researchers are currently testing four medicines—phenylbutyrate, milrinone, genistein, and CPX—for this purpose.

Scientists have developed a drug to thin the mucus and make it less sticky. This makes breathing easier. Researchers are working on other drugs to relieve the symptoms in people with CF.

Avenues for Research: Better Therapy Devices

Some researchers work to find better therapy devices for people with cystic fibrosis. One device is called the flutter. It's small, held in the hand, and looks like a pipe. To use it, people exhale through the flutter. A special valve in the device causes fast air pressure movements in the airways. This moves mucus out from the airways. Then it's coughed up and out. People can use a flutter by themselves, so it gives them more independence. Mechanical vibration devices called vests also are useful in removing thick mucus from the lungs.

Clinical Trials

People with CF can help advance knowledge about the disease. They can do this by participating in clinical trials. These studies find better ways to prevent, diagnose, or treat a disease. Many clinical trials involve testing new drugs or combinations of drugs. Others may involve gene therapy. Clinical trials follow strict scientific procedures.

People need to think carefully before deciding to join a clinical trial. They may benefit from the new treatment. However, risks usually are involved in something new and experimental. Most of today's effective treatments resulted from clinical trials. Participants may not benefit directly. However, they can have satisfaction in knowing they have helped others.

Craig has mild cystic fibrosis. So far, doctors have managed to control his disease fairly well. Now Craig wants to do more. While on the Internet, he found information about a gene therapy study. The study would be conducted at a medical school near his home. The medical school would pay all his expenses for the study.

Craig, Age 18

Craig talked with his own doctor and his parents first. Then, he gave his medical reports to the study's doctors. They said he qualified. His gene therapy study was done over three separate times: once in April, then in July, and finally in October. Each was from four to six weeks long.

The study results showed promise. Craig said, "I felt proud to be doing something to help fight cystic fibrosis."

Points to Consider

How could your school help raise money for cystic fibrosis research?

What could you do to educate other people about cystic fibrosis?

Would you participate in a clinical trial? Why or why not?

If someone you know were diagnosed with CF and wanted to try an unproven treatment, how would you react?

Glossary

bronchial tube (BRONG-kee-uhl TOOB)—one of two main divisions of the trachea, or windpipe; the two bronchial tubes lead into the lungs.

bronchodilator (brong-koh-dye-LAY-tur)—a drug that widens the breathing tubes to make breathing easier

carrier (KAR-ee-ur)—a person who has the gene to pass a genetic disease to his or her children; usually a carrier has no symptoms of the disease.

chronic (KRON-ik)—continuing for a long time; a person with a chronic disease or illness may have it throughout life.

decongestant (dee-kuhn-JESS-tuhnt)—a medicine that shrinks the blood vessels in the nose to help a person breathe more easily

enzyme (EN-zime)—a protein in the body that causes chemical reactions

gene (JEEN)—the basic unit of heredity that determines how a person looks and grows

inflammation (in-fluh-MAY-shuhn)—redness, swelling, heat, and pain; people with cystic fibrosis often have inflamed airways.

mucolytic (myoo-kuh-LI-tik)—a drug that thins mucus, which makes it easier for mucus to drain from the body

mucus (MYOO-kuhss)—clear, slippery liquid that coats, cleans, and protects the inside of the mouth, nose, throat, and other breathing passages

pancreas (PAN-kree-uhss)—a gland near the stomach that produces enzymes to help digest food

respiratory system (RESS-pi-ruh-taw-ree SISS-tuhm)—the group of body parts, including the lungs, that allows a person to breathe

tract (TRAKT)—a group of body parts or organs that performs a specific function

For More Information

Deford, Frank. *Alex: The Life of a Child.* Nashville, TN: Rutledge Hill, 1997.

Huegel, Kelly. *Young People and Chronic Illness: True Stories, Help, and Hope.* Minneapolis: Free Spirit, 1998.

LeVert, Suzanne. *Teens Face to Face With Chronic Illness.* New York: Julian Messner, 1993.

Silverstein, Alvin, Virginia Silverstein, and Robert Silverstein. *Cystic Fibrosis.* New York: Franklin Watts, 1994.

Note At publication, all resources listed here were accurate and appropriate to the topics covered in this book. Addresses and phone numbers may change. When visiting Internet sites and links, use good judgment. Remember, never give personal information over the Internet.

Useful Addresses and Internet Sites

Canadian Cystic Fibrosis Foundation (CCFF)
2221 Yonge Street, Suite 601
Toronto, ON M4S 2B4
CANADA
1-800-378-CCFF (800-378-2233) (Canada only)
www.ccff.ca

Cystic Fibrosis Foundation (CFF)
6931 Arlington Road, #200
Bethesda, MD 20814
1-800-FIGHT-CF (800-344-4823)
www.cff.org

Cystic Fibrosis Research Inc.
Bayside Business Plaza
2672 Bayshore Parkway, Suite 520
Mountain View, CA 94043
www.cfri.org

International Association of Cystic Fibrosis
Adults (IACFA)
Barbara Palys
82 Ayer Road
Harvard, MA 01451
www.iacfa.org

National Heart, Lung, and Blood Health
Information Center (NHLBHI)
PO Box 30105
Bethesda, MD 20824-0105
*www.nhlbi.nih.gov/health/public/lung/other/
cystfib.htm*

Second Wind Lung Transplant Association, Inc.
300 South Duncan Avenue, Suite 227
Clearwater, FL 33755-6457
1-888-855-9463
www.2ndwind.org

Cystic Fibrosis USA
www.cfusa.org
Has an information center and game gallery
both related to cystic fibrosis

CysticFibrosis.com
www.cysticfibrosis.com
Is an online community with information and
chat about cystic fibrosis; includes a just-for-
kids section.

KidsHealth
www.kidshealth.org
Provides easy-to-understand information on
a variety of health topics, including cystic
fibrosis

Index

Andersen, Dorothy H., 10
antibiotics, 30, 49, 57
asthma, 5, 23, 26

bacteria, 6, 15, 26, 57
breathing, 9, 15, 24, 25, 29, 30, 57
bronchial tubes, 14, 15
bronchiectasis, 15
bronchioles, 14, 15
bronchitis, 15
bronchodilators, 30, 31

calories, 33, 34, 35, 38
Canadian Cystic Fibrosis Foundation
    (CCFF), 40
carriers, 8
CFTR protein, 7, 57
chest physical therapy (CPT), 30, 31, 39
chest X rays, 26, 27
chloride, 7, 25, 26, 27, 57. *See also* salt
clinical trials, 58–59
coughing, 9, 10, 15, 21, 22, 31, 46, 47,
    48, 49, 58
CPX, 57
cystic fibrosis
    causes of, 6
    coping with, 51–53
    defined, 6–7
    diagnosing, 23–26
    managing, 29–35
    research on, 55–59
    symptoms of, 10, 15–17, 21–23
    treating, 24, 29, 30–34, 38, 47, 51,
        55
    who gets it, 8–9
Cystic Fibrosis Foundation (CFF), 40,
    59
Cystic Fibrosis Research, Inc. (CFRI),
    40
Cystic Fibrosis Scholarship
    Foundation, 50

death (from cystic fibrosis), 15, 17, 24
decongestants, 30, 31
dehydration, 11, 16, 22
diabetes, 14
diet, 10, 33–34
dietitians, 35, 38
digestive system, 6, 9, 10, 13, 16, 23,
    29
digestive treatment, 33–34
doctors, 24, 26, 27, 29, 35, 38, 40, 51,
    52
drugs, 57, 58. *See also* medicines

electric chest clappers, 30
emotions, 38, 39, 42, 49
energy, lack of, 22
enzymes, 16, 33, 49, 51
exercise, 9, 31–32, 33, 52
exhaustion, 22

family, 35, 37, 39, 42, 43, 49, 50
finger clubbing, 22
fitting in, 47
flutter, 58
friends, 42, 43, 48, 50

gene testing, 26
gene therapy, 56, 57, 58
genetics, 6, 7, 8–9. *See also* inherited
        diseases
genistein, 57

height, 22
hospital staff, 39

ibuprofen, 57
independence, 50
infections, 16, 22, 24, 30, 33
inflammation, 57
inherited diseases, 11. *See also*
        genetics

Index continued

International Association of Cystic Fibrosis Adults (IACFA), 40
Internet, 52, 53

kyphosis, 19

larynx (voice box), 14, 15
life expectancy, 6, 55
lung disease, 15
lung infections, 9, 10, 15, 22, 30
lung transplants, 34
lung treatment, 30–32
lungs, 6, 7, 9, 10, 13–15, 26, 56

macrolides, 57
medicines, 30–31, 47, 48, 49, 51. *See also* drugs
mental health counselors, 39
milrinone, 57
minerals, 17
mucolytics, 30, 31
mucus, 6, 7, 14, 15, 17, 26, 30, 31, 57, 58

nasal polyps, 22
nebulizers, 31, 39
nose drops, 56
nurses, 35, 38, 42, 51

organizations, 40, 52, 62

pancreas, 6, 7, 10, 14, 16, 33
pancreas tests, 26
phenylbutyrate, 57
physical development, 45–46
pregnancy, 17–18, 46–47
pulmonary function tests, 26

reproductive system, 9, 13, 17
research, 55–59
respiratory system, 9, 13–15
respiratory therapists, 35, 39

salt, 7, 9, 11, 16, 23, 24, 32, 34, 56, 57. *See also* chloride
school, 5, 48, 58
sex hormones, 17
sexuality, 46–47
sexually transmitted diseases, 46–47
sinus infections, 22
skin, 11, 22, 25
small intestine, 9, 33
social workers, 35, 39–40
spine, 19
sputum tests, 26
stools, 22
stress, 37, 39
support, 36–43
support groups, 40, 41, 50, 52, 53
sweat, 11, 17, 24, 26, 27, 34
sweat glands, 9, 13, 16–17
sweat test, 24, 25, 26

testes, 17
therapy devices, 58
trachea (windpipe), 14, 15

vibrating vests, 30, 32, 50, 58
vitamins, 33, 34, 49

weight, 16, 21, 22, 23, 47